577.34   Fleisher, Paul
FLE   Forest food webs in action

DATE DUE			
OC 7 2 '15			

ANNIE E VINTON ELEMENTARY
SCHOOL LIBRARY
306 STAFFORD ROAD
MANSFIELD CENTER, CT 06250

Searchlight

What
Is a
Food Web?

Forest Food Webs
in Action

Paul Fleisher

Lerner Publications Company
Minneapolis

Lerner Publications Company
A division of Lerner Publishing Group, Inc.
241 First Avenue North
Minneapolis, MN 55401 U.S.A.

Website address: www.lernerbooks.com

Library of Congress Cataloging-in-Publication Data

Fleisher, Paul.
    Forest food webs in action / by Paul Fleisher.
        p.   cm. — (Searchlight books™—what is a food web?)
    Includes index.
    ISBN 978-1-4677-1254-5 (lib. bdg. : alk. paper)
    ISBN 978-1-4677-1774-8 (eBook)
    1. Forest ecology—Juvenile literature. 2. Forest plants—Juvenile literature.
    3. Forest animals—Juvenile literature. I. Title.
    QH541.5.F6F58 2014
    577.3—dc23   2012032546

Manufactured in the United States of America
1 – BP – 7/15/13

Contents

A FOREST FOOD WEB

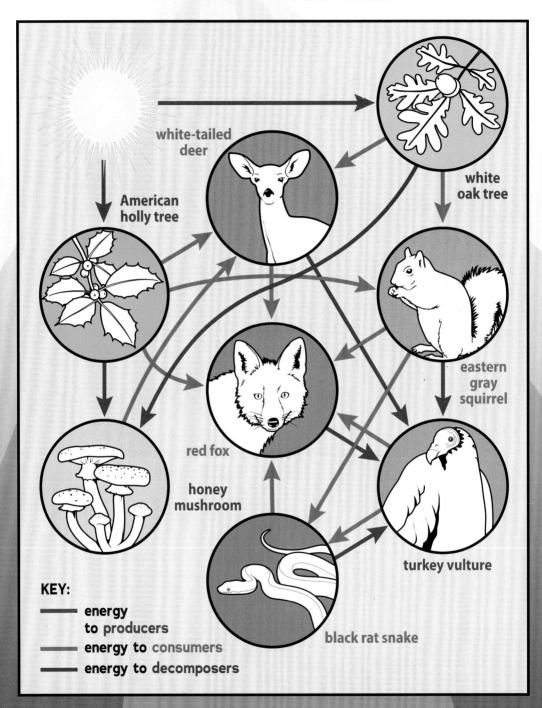

white-tailed deer

white oak tree

American holly tree

eastern gray squirrel

red fox

honey mushroom

turkey vulture

black rat snake

KEY:
— energy to producers
— energy to consumers
— energy to decomposers

Chapter 1

FORESTS

Tall trees tower above you. Fallen leaves cover the ground. Small plants grow in the shade beneath the trees. You are in a forest. Forests are also called woodlands, or woods.

Forests are places where lots of trees and plants grow. What is another name for forests?

What Lives in a Forest?

Forests have many trees. They also have bushes, ferns, and mushrooms. Insects and mice live here. So do deer and raccoons. Tiny bacteria live in the soil. Bacteria are much too small for us to see.

Many different kinds of plants live on the forest floor.

Red foxes live in forests. Foxes eat other animals. This fox has caught an animal to eat.

Forests are some of Earth's most important environments. An environment is the place where any creature lives. The environment includes the air, soil, weather, and other plants and animals.

Linked Together

Plants and animals in the forest are linked to one another. They depend on one another. Some animals eat living plants. Some creatures eat dead wood and leaves. Other animals are meat eaters. They eat other animals. When plants and animals die, they break down into chemicals. The chemicals become part of the soil. Some of these chemicals help plants grow.

This is a dead tree. The tree's wood is breaking down. It will become part of the soil.

Energy moves from one living thing to another. A food chain shows how the energy moves. The energy for life comes from the sun. Plants store the sun's energy in their leaves, stems, and roots. When an animal eats a plant, the animal gets some of the sun's energy from the plant. The energy moves farther along the food chain each time one living thing eats another.

THIS MOTH CATERPILLAR HAS EATEN MOST OF THE LEAF.

Many Food Chains

A forest has many food chains. Imagine that a caterpillar eats a leaf. Then a bird eats the caterpillar. A bobcat eats the bird. When the bobcat dies, a vulture eats its body. The sun's energy passes from the leaf to the caterpillar. Then it passes to the bird. Then it goes to the bobcat. Then it goes to the vulture.

A gray catbird is feeding a caterpillar to its babies.

But birds don't eat only caterpillars. They also eat seeds, beetles, and worms. Bobcats eat other things besides birds. Bobcats also eat rabbits, squirrels, and mice. And vultures eat all kinds of dead animals. An environment's food web is made up of many food chains. A food web shows how all living things depend on one another for food.

This bird is a Swainson's thrush. It is eating a berry. It also eats beetles, ants, caterpillars, and other foods.

Chapter 2

FOREST PLANTS

Green plants use sunlight to make food. Because plants produce food, they are called producers. Plants also make oxygen. Oxygen is a gas in the air. All animals need oxygen to breathe.

A forest's energy comes from the sun. Plants use sunlight to make food. What else do plants make?

Photosynthesis

The way plants make food and oxygen is called photosynthesis. Plants need carbon dioxide, sunlight, and water for photosynthesis. Carbon dioxide is another gas in the air. A plant's leaves take in carbon dioxide and sunlight. The plant's roots take in water. The plant uses energy from sunlight to turn the carbon dioxide and water into sugar and starch. Sugar and starch are the plant's own food. The plant stores this food in its leaves and roots.

HOW PHOTOSYNTHESIS WORKS

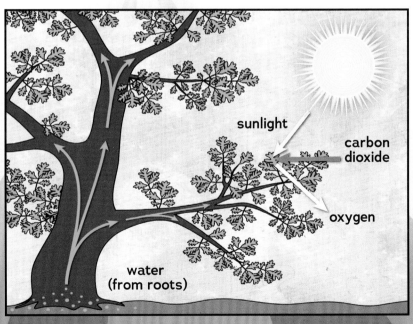

sunlight

carbon dioxide

oxygen

water (from roots)

An oak tree's leaves turn sunlight, carbon dioxide, and water into food for the tree.

As the plant makes food, it also makes oxygen. The oxygen goes into the air. Animals breathe in the oxygen. They breathe out carbon dioxide. Plants use the carbon dioxide to make more food.

All animals breathe oxygen. This animal is a white-tailed deer.

Nutrients

Plants grow in soil. The soil contains chemicals called nutrients. Living things need nutrients to grow. When it rains, water soaks into the soil. Nutrients from the soil go into the water. When a plant's roots take in the water, the plant gets nutrients from the soil too. The nutrients become part of the plant.

A tree's roots grow deep into the ground. The roots take in water and nutrients from the soil.

Forest Layers

Trees are the largest plants in a forest. The branches of large trees spread high above the ground. The trees' branches and leaves are called the canopy. The leaves in the canopy get plenty of sunlight for making food. But the canopy keeps sunlight from reaching the ground.

A forest's canopy blocks most of the light from the sun.

Young trees are called saplings. Saplings grow on the forest floor. They grow from seeds that fell from older trees. Most saplings die. Many don't get enough light to grow. Others are eaten by animals.

Most saplings grow under older trees.

Smaller plants live in forests too. They make up the part of the forest called the understory. Plants in the understory live in the shade of the big trees. But most of these plants don't need much sunlight to live. Blueberry bushes grow in the understory. Mosses, ferns, and flowers grow there too.

Smaller forest plants make up the understory.

When a big tree dies, it falls down. It leaves an open space in the canopy. The open space is called a clearing. In a clearing, sunlight can reach the forest floor. Saplings can gather a lot of sunlight. They grow quickly. But only a few of them will live long enough to become big trees.

Spaces between trees let sunlight reach the ground.

Chapter 3

FOREST PLANT EATERS

Animals are called consumers. *Consume* means "eat." Animals that eat plants are called herbivores. The sun's energy is stored inside plants. When an animal eats a plant, it gets the sun's energy.

This young porcupine is eating tree bark. What are some other animals that eat plants?

Many insects are herbivores. Caterpillars munch on leaves. Leafhoppers suck juices from plants. Bees get their food from flowers.

Some beetles lay eggs under the bark of trees. Grubs hatch from the eggs. Grubs look like short, fat worms. The grubs burrow under the bark. They eat the wood.

The bark has come off this dead tree. Beetle grubs used to live under the bark. The lines in the wood are tunnels that the grubs made.

Many kinds of birds eat plants. Chickadees eat seeds. Bluebirds eat berries. Wild turkeys eat acorns, seeds, and fruit.

Wild turkeys are looking for food in a forest clearing.

Mammals are animals with hair that feed their babies milk. Many mammals are herbivores. Mice eat seeds, leaves, roots, and bark. Chipmunks eat nuts and fruit. Deer, moose, and elk are the largest plant eaters in the forest. They munch on leaves and twigs.

This moose is eating willow leaves.

Moving Seeds

Plants can't move around. Many of their seeds fall straight down to the ground. When the seeds sprout, the growing plants are in the shade. They don't get enough light to grow well. Animals help to move plants' seeds from place to place.

Nuts are tree seeds. Gray squirrels bury nuts to eat later. But the squirrels forget about some of the nuts. The forgotten nuts may grow into new trees.

In a different place, the new plants may be able to grow better. Ants and squirrels hide seeds to eat later. Some of the seeds sprout before the animals come back to eat them. When birds eat fruit, seeds from the fruit end up in the birds' droppings. Some of those seeds sprout too.

Berries have seeds inside them. When a bird eats berries, the seeds pass through its body. When the bird's droppings fall on the ground, the seeds may sprout.

Chapter 4

FOREST MEAT EATERS

Some forest creatures eat meat. These animals are called carnivores. Carnivores eat animals. But they need plants too. Carnivores get energy by eating animals that have eaten plants. Spiders are carnivores. Some spiders weave sticky webs. They use the webs to catch flying insects.

This spider is a carnivore. What is a carnivore?

Insects can be carnivores too. Wasps capture insects to feed to their young. Ants also hunt and eat other insects.

Toads hide in damp leaves on the forest floor. They hunt earthworms and insects. Black rat snakes climb high into the trees. They search for bird eggs and chicks to eat. They also eat other small animals, such as mice.

RAT SNAKES ARE GOOD AT CLIMBING TREES.

Some birds are carnivores. Owls catch mice and rats. Bald eagles eat fish and small mammals.

Many mammals are carnivores too. Foxes eat mice, birds, and snakes. Opossums eat insects, rabbits, and worms.

Opossums hunt small animals such as insects and worms. But they also eat meat from animals that have already died. This opossum is eating a rabbit.

Omnivores

Some animals eat both plants and meat. These animals are called omnivores. Raccoons eat frogs, snakes, birds, small mammals, nuts, and fruit. Bears are the largest omnivores in the forest. They eat deer, fish, insects, roots, and berries.

Black bears eat both animals and plants. This bear is eating fruit from a tree.

Chapter 5

FOREST DECOMPOSERS

All living things die. When plants and animals die, they decay. They break down into nutrients. Living things called decomposers help dead things decay. Decomposers feed on dead plants and animals.

This dead tree has fallen down. Many dead trees fall down every year. Why isn't the ground covered with dead trees?

Nature's Recyclers

Decomposers are nature's recyclers. They break down dead plants and animals. Nutrients from the dead plants and animals go into the soil. Then other living things can use the nutrients.

Decomposers are very important. Without them, forests would be filled with dead plants and animals. Then no new plants could grow. Animals would run out of food.

Tiny bacteria are breaking down these dead leaves. Nutrients from the leaves will go into the soil.

Many insects are decomposers. Termites live in the wood of dead trees. They eat the wood. They slowly turn the trees into soil. Some beetles and flies lay their eggs on dead animals. When the young insects hatch, they feed on the dead bodies. This helps break down the bodies into soil as well.

Pill bugs are decomposers. They are also called sow bugs or wood lice.

Mushrooms and other fungi are decomposers too. Fungi get their food from dead leaves and wood. Many different kinds of fungi live in forests.

Bacteria also feed on dead plants and animals. Bacteria are all around us. But they are so tiny we cannot see them.

FUNGI ARE GROWING ON A ROTTING LOG.

Chapter 6

PEOPLE AND FORESTS

Many people like to visit forests. People hike and camp in the woods. They enjoy watching forest animals and sitting under shady trees.

This mother and child are exploring a forest. Why do people like to visit forests?

Cutting Down Trees

People use forests for other things too. People cut down trees. They use wood from the trees to build houses. They also make wood into paper.

After trees are cut down, new trees grow. But trees grow slowly. It takes many years for a forest to grow. When a forest's trees are cut down, animals that lived in the trees must find new homes.

Part of this forest was cut down. People have planted new trees. The trees will take a long time to grow tall.

Forest Fires

Sometimes fires start in forests. A fire may start when lightning strikes a tree. People cause forest fires too. They may be careless with matches. Or they may forget to put out a campfire. Fire can help a forest. It burns away dead leaves and fallen branches. It makes room for new plants to grow. But fire is harmful too. Forest fires destroy many trees and other plants. They kill woodland animals.

A fire burned down many trees in this forest. But new trees have sprouted. Very slowly, the forest is growing back.

Protecting Forests

Much of the United States was once covered with forests. But people cut down many trees to make space for cities and farms. Protecting the woodlands means protecting forest food webs. It means protecting everything that lives in a forest.

FORESTS ARE HOME TO MANY DIFFERENT KINDS OF PLANTS AND ANIMALS.

Glossary

bacteria: tiny living things made up of just one cell. Bacteria can be seen only under a microscope.

canopy: the branches and leaves of the large trees in a forest

carnivore: an animal that eats meat

consumer: a living thing that eats other living things. Animals are consumers.

decay: to break down

decomposer: a living thing that feeds on dead plants and animals

environment: a place where creatures live. An environment includes the air, soil, weather, plants, and animals in a place.

food chain: the way energy moves from the sun to a plant, then to a plant eater, then to a meat eater, and finally to a decomposer

food web: many food chains connected together. A food web shows how all living things in a place need one another for food.

herbivore: an animal that eats plants

nutrient: a chemical that a living thing needs to grow

omnivore: an animal that eats both plants and meat

photosynthesis: the way green plants use energy from sunlight to make their own food out of carbon dioxide and water

producer: a living thing that makes its own food. Plants are producers.

understory: the small trees, bushes, and other plants that live under the tall trees in a forest

LERNER

Expand learning beyond the printed book. Download free, complementary educational resources for this book from our website, www.lernersource.com.

SOURCE

Learn More about Forests and Food Webs

Books

Latham, Donna. *Rain Forests.* White River Junction, VT: Nomad Press, 2011. Learn about rain forest landscape, climate, plants, animals, and more.

Wojahn, Rebecca Hogue, and Donald Wojahn. *A Temperate Forest Food Chain: A Who-Eats-What Adventure in North America.* Minneapolis: Lerner Publications Company, 2009. What you choose to eat shapes your fate in this fun interactive story about food chains.

Zoehfeld, Kathleen Weidner. *Secrets of the Garden: Food Chains and the Food Web in Our Backyard.* New York: Alfred A. Knopf, 2012. This book takes a fun approach to examining food chains and the food web that exist in one family's backyard garden.

Websites

All about Rainforests

http://www.enchantedlearning.com/subjects/rainforest

This colorful site has information on some of the plants and animals that live in rain forests, plus quizzes, activities, and more.

Chain Reaction

http://www.ecokids.ca/pub/eco_info/topics/frogs/chain_reaction/index.cfm#

Create a food chain and find out what happens if one link is taken out of the chain.

Food Chains and Food Webs

http://www.vtaide.com/png/foodchains.htm

This website has an interactive tool to let you create your own food webs.

Smokey Kids

http://www.smokeybear.com/kids/?js=1

This page has forest facts, information on forest fires, games, and more.

Index

Photo Acknowledgments

The images in this book are used with the permission of: © Zeke Smith/Independent Picture Service, pp. 4, 13; © Photodisc/Getty Images, pp. 5, 18, 22, 26, 33, 37; © Todd Strand/Independent Picture Service, pp. 6, 12, 15, 30, 31; Robin West/U.S. Fish and Wildlife Service, p. 7; © Martin Plsek/Shutterstock.com, p. 8; Scott Bauer/Agricultural Research Service, USDA, p. 9; © Bill Beatty/Visuals Unlimited, Inc., p. 10; © Steve Maslowski/Visuals Unlimited, Inc., p. 11; © Tom Reichner/Shutterstock.com, p. 14; © Ioan Panaite/Shutterstock.com, p. 16; © iStockphoto.com/Michael Krinke, p. 17; © Andreas Altenburger/Shutterstock.com, p. 19; © Alain/Dreamstime.com, p. 20; © Alexey Antipov/Dreamstime.com, p. 21; © Warren Price/Dreamstime.com, p. 23; © Richard Parsons/Dreamstime.com, p. 24; U.S. Fish and Wildlife Service, p. 25; © Matt Jeppson/Shutterstock.com, p. 27; © Joe McDonald/CORBIS, p. 28; © Lynn Amaral/Shutterstock.com, p. 29; © iStockphoto.com/Wayne Stadler, p. 32; © iStockphoto.com/lostinbids, p. 34; © iStockphoto.com/georgeclerk, p. 35; © iStockphoto.com/epicurean, p. 36.

Front Cover: © Tosca Weijers/Dreamstime.com.

Main body text set in Adrianna Regular 14/20.
Typeface provided by Chank.